SPOTLIGHT ON NATIONS

CHINA

NELL MUSOLF

CREATIVE EDUCATION · CREATIVE PAPERBACKS

Published by Creative Education and Creative Paperbacks
P.O. Box 227, Mankato, Minnesota 56002
Creative Education and Creative Paperbacks are imprints of The Creative Company
www.thecreativecompany.us

Design and production by Blue Design, Inc.
Art direction by Graham Morgan
Edited by Grace Beltowski and Ana Brauer

Photographs by Getty Images/Bettmann, 12, Chen Xiao/VCG, 27, Edwin Tan, 21, Mo Guibin/VCG, 18; Pexels/ Ella Wei, 9, Paulo Marcelo Martins, cover, 1, SAM LIM, 4–5, Manglietia, 14; Unsplash/Edward He, 24, Joey Huang, 16, Nuno Alberto, 28, Weichao Deng, 23, Zheng Wuji, 29; Wikimedia Commons/British Museum/public domain, 11, Jakub Hałun, 3, lol1VNIO, 15, National Geographic/public domain, 6, Nir B. Gurung, 10, public domain, 17, RootOfAllLight, 26, Zeng Liansong, 8, 10, 14, 16, 20, 22

Library of Congress Cataloging-in-Publication Data
Names: Musolf, Nell author
Title: China / by Nell Musolf.
Description: Mankato, Minnesota : Creative Education and Creative Paperbacks, [2026] | Series: Spotlight on nations | Includes bibliographical references and index. | Audience: Ages 10–13 | Audience: Grades 4–6 | Summary: "Explore China's history, culture, political evolution, economic growth, environmental challenges, and future goals like space exploration and social issues. Written for middle-grade readers, this book includes timelines, sidebars, glossary, resources, and index"—Provided by publisher.
Identifiers: LCCN 2025016991 (print) | LCCN 2025016992 (ebook) | ISBN 9798895810699 library binding | ISBN 9798896800224 paperback | ISBN 9798895811955 ebook
Subjects: LCSH: China—Juvenile literature | China—Civilization | China—History | China—Politics and government | China—Description and travel
Classification: LCC DS706 .M88 2026 (print) | LCC DS706 (ebook) | DDC 951—dc23/eng/20250528
LC record available at https://lccn.loc.gov/2025016991
LC ebook record available at https://lccn.loc.gov/2025016992

Printed in the United States

CONTENTS

INTRODUCTION

DISCOVERING CHINA

China is one of the oldest countries in the world. The history of China goes back more than 4,000 years. Many people live there. One out of every five people on the planet are Chinese. China is a big country, so big that it covers almost all the land in East Asia. Since China is such a large country, it has several different climates. There are mountains, deserts, and plains, each with a unique landscape. Exotic animals like red pandas and clouded leopards live there. Chinese alligators and Asian elephants can also be found. China's natural resources include coal, oil, minerals, and metals. There are manmade treasures, too, including the Great Wall, jade coffins found in ancient tombs, and pieces of porcelain dating back thousands of years. China is a fascinating country filled with people who love their home and are proud of their long history.

CLOSE-UP

Qin Shi Huang

Qin Shi Huang lived from 259 to 210 BC. Before he ruled, China was made up of many warring states. He conquered them all and became the first emperor of a united China. His huge tomb includes thousands of life-sized clay soldiers, called terracotta warriors, that were meant to protect him in the afterlife.

CHAPTER ONE

CHINA THROUGH THE AGES

Archaeologists have found human fossils in China showing people lived in the region more than a million years ago. Those early people were hunter-gatherers. Later, the Chinese were ruled by **dynasties**. The first empire was the Qin dynasty. It began in 221 B.C. Several other dynasties followed the Qin dynasty. China became a **republic** in 1912. In 1940, China became a **communist** country. It has remained communist since then.

Trading goods with other countries was a crucial part of the early Chinese economy. Silk was one of the first items traded. A route called the Silk Road was used to transport silk from China to traders in other countries. The Silk Road wasn't a single road. It was made up of several roads linking China to various regions, including the Roman Empire, Central Asia, the Middle East, and Europe. The Chinese traded silk to the west. In return, they received woolen products, as well as gold and silver, from western countries. Material goods weren't the only things that were carried from the east to the west.

MILESTONES IN CHINA'S HISTORY

2200 B.C.
- Founding of Hsai dynasty

1000 B.C.
- People begin weaving silk and making maps

Ideas and religions such as Christianity and Buddhism also traveled along the Silk Road.

The people of China have invented many different items. Paper is one of the most important things invented by the Chinese. The first paper was made in 105 A.D. After paper, the Chinese invented **movable type** printing. This made it possible to print books and share ideas with the rest of the world. The compass is another important Chinese invention. It was first used for *feng shui*, a practice that helps arrange buildings in harmony with nature. Compasses helped Chinese ships navigate the oceans. Clocks, umbrellas, porcelain, and toothbrushes were also invented in China.

China has experienced many natural disasters throughout its history. Floods, earthquakes, and fires have killed millions of people. Some of the disasters have led to widespread **famine**. In response, the people of China

CLOSE-UP

Railroads

The railroad system in China is so long that if all the railway lines were put together, they could loop around Earth two times.

The Great Wall

The Great Wall of China took thousands of years to build. It isn't one continuous wall. It is a series of walls that stretches from Mount Hu in the east to Jiayu Pass in the west. The Wall is 13,271 miles (21,196 kilometers) long. It moves up and down the hillsides like a long, wriggly centipede. For many years, people thought the Great Wall could be seen from space, but astronauts have said that this is not true. Even so, the Wall is still one of the longest and oldest man-made structures on the planet.

tried to learn from what happened so they could prevent it from happening again. The Three Gorges Dam was built to provide protection from flooding. Construction began in 1994 and was completed in 2006. It remains one of the largest engineering projects in China's history.

During the 20th century, China changed a great deal. It went from being ruled by dynasties to having a communist government. Since the 1970s, China has seen a huge amount of economic growth. It manufactures materials that are sent all over the world. However, making so many products has caused pollution problems. China is working to fix those problems, but it takes time. With such a large population to support, the Chinese government knows it will always have a challenge keeping its people healthy and well fed while also keeping the environment healthy.

800-900 AD

- Newspapers and books begin to be created

1271

- Marco Polo first visits China

CLOSE-UP

Everest

The tallest mountain in the world is on the border of China and Nepal. Mount Everest is 29,000 feet (8,848 meters) tall. That's a long way to the top!

HISTORICAL  HIGHLIGHT

Feng Shui

Feng shui is the art of arranging things in a certain way to bring about peace and harmony. The ancient Chinese created feng shui more than 6,000 years ago. Feng shui means "the way of wind and water" in Chinese. The ancient Chinese believed everything has a life force. By balancing objects in a certain way, the life force could be positive or negative. People thought that arranging items in a positive way would bring health, friendships, good luck, and money.

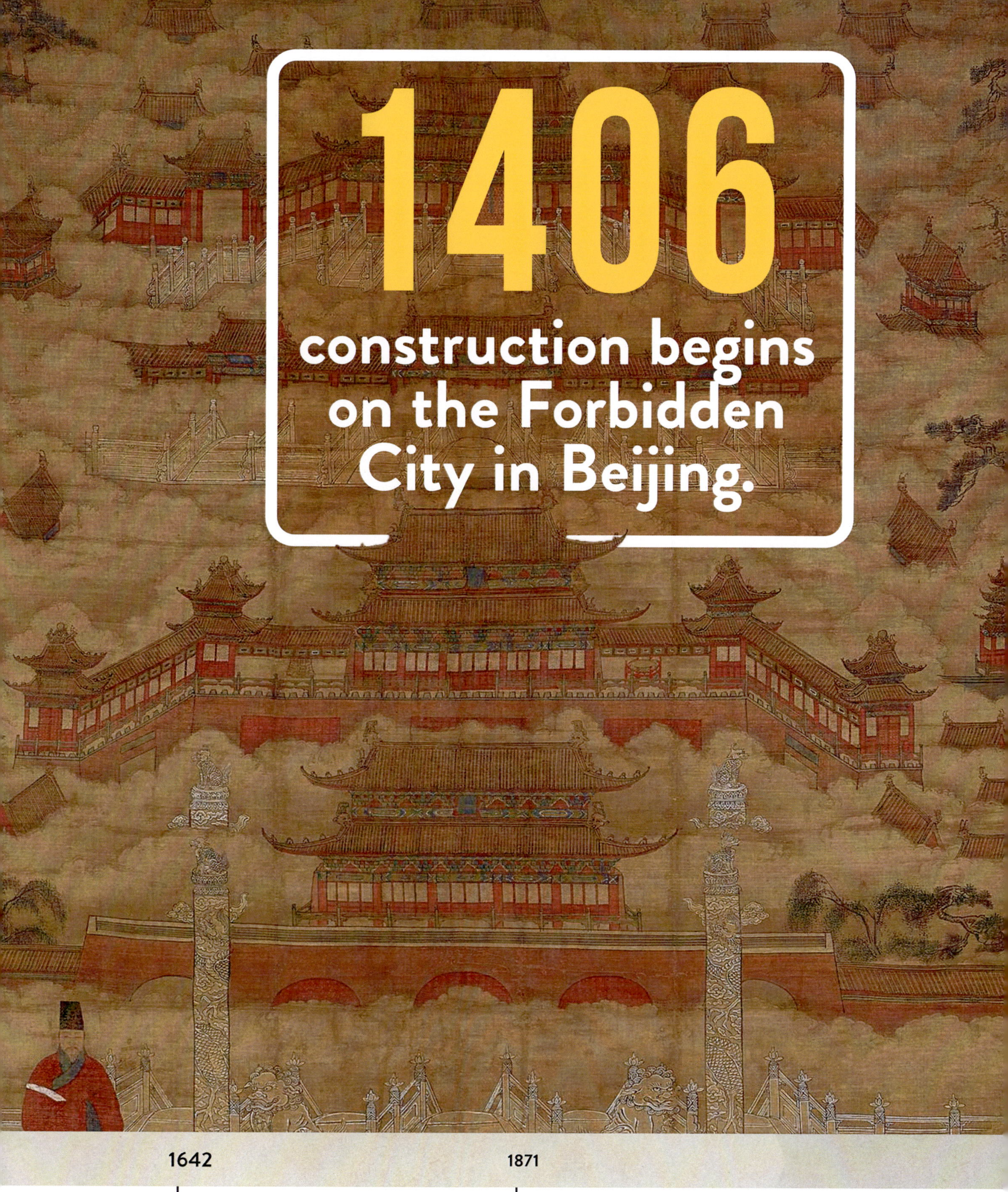

1406

construction begins on the Forbidden City in Beijing.

1642

- Flood in northern China kills 900,000 people

1871

- American president Abraham Lincoln authorizes mail service to China

CLOSE-UP

Mao

Mao Zedong rose to prominence as a leader within the Chinese Communist Party (CCP) in 1943. He later played a pivotal role in the establishment of the People's Republic of China in 1949, serving as its chairman until his death in 1976.

CHAPTER TWO

POLITICAL HISTORY

The government of China has changed a great deal since its early days of dynasty rule. The early part of the 20th century had many conflicts between people who wanted China to become communist and people who wanted it to be a republic.

The fights ended when Mao Zedong took control of the country in 1949. That was when China became a communist country and an **authoritarian** state. It officially became known as the People's Republic of China.

The Chinese government is very powerful, and citizens must follow the rules it sets. For many years, the government was able to control almost everything people did. For example, families could have only one child. This was an effort to control **overpopulation**. The government changed the rule in 2015. Now families can have up to three children.

In its early years, China was an agricultural country. Under the leadership of Chairman Mao, China moved from farming to industry. To grow enough

1894

- China goes to war with Japan

1921

- Chinese Communist Party is founded

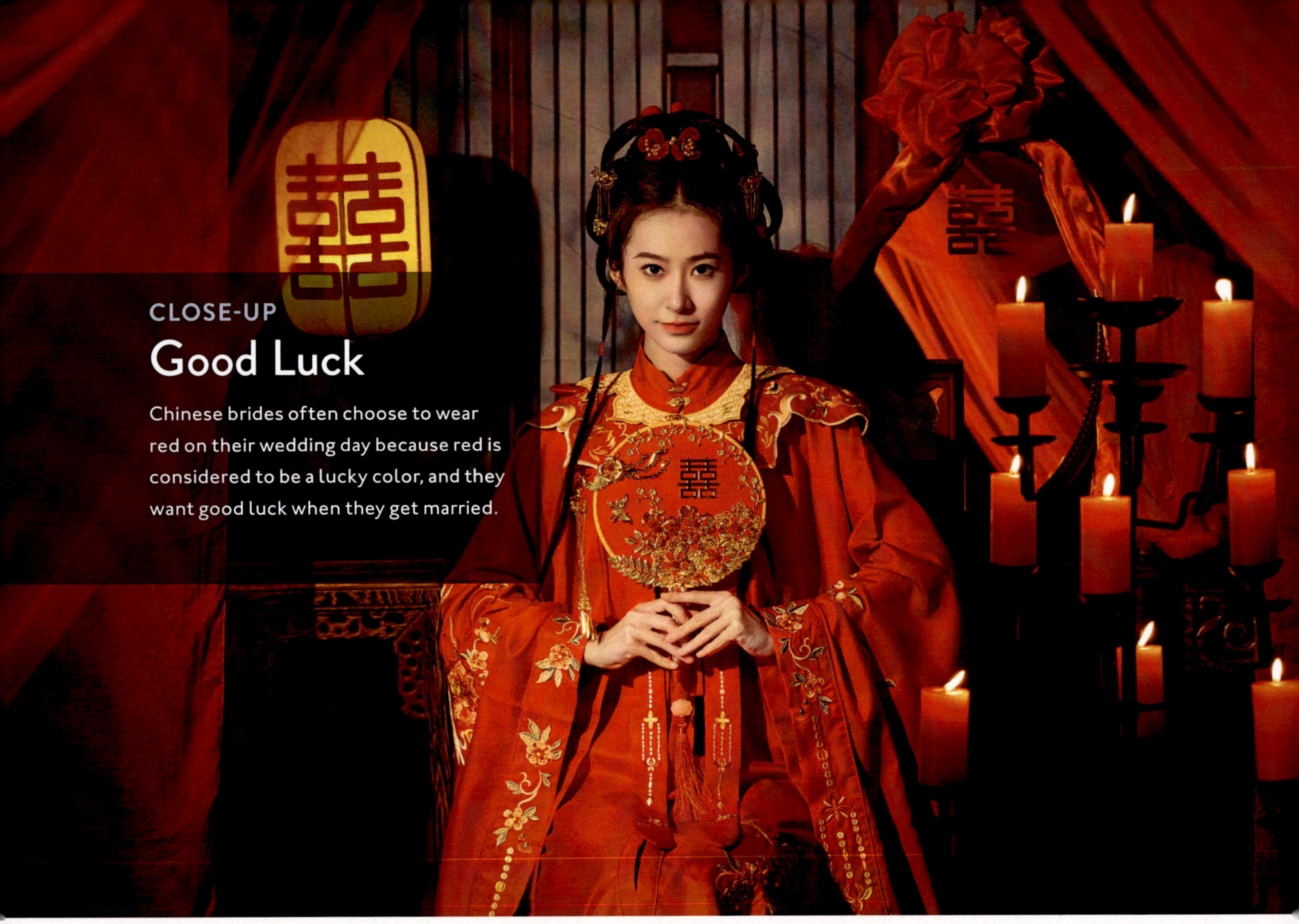

CLOSE-UP

Good Luck

Chinese brides often choose to wear red on their wedding day because red is considered to be a lucky color, and they want good luck when they get married.

HISTORICAL  HIGHLIGHT

Communal Living

Chairman Mao wanted to get rid of the traditional family structure. He believed families kept poor people from improving their lives. He came up with a plan to change how Chinese people lived. His plan was to make peasants give their farmland to the government and live together in **communes**. The idea behind communal living is for everyone to work together and share what they have. People ate in cafeterias so homes would not need kitchens. Children were put in daycare centers instead of being cared for by their family. There was very little privacy. Communal living ultimately failed, and families are again important in China.

food for the people, communes were formed, and peasants were forced to work on them instead of owning their own land. The plan was a failure that resulted in famine and 56 million deaths.

After Mao's death in 1976, Deng Xiaoping became China's chairman. During his time of leadership, many people were not happy with the government. Students especially did not like how the country was being run. They wanted the freedom to speak without fear, and they wanted newspapers to be able to print the truth. The 1989 democracy movement brought together people who were fighting for those freedoms. They met in Tiananmen Square, a city square in the center of Beijing, and they protested against the government. The protests started in April 1989 and ended June 4, when the government declared **martial law**. More than 300 protesters were killed in what became known as the Tiananmen Square Massacre.

China's current leader, Xi Jinping, has served as China's president since 2013. He was elected to a third five-year term in 2023. Under his leadership, China has grown steadily. China has the world's fastest growing economy in the 21st century. Its **gross domestic product (GDP)** doubled between 2002 and 2006. A country's GDP is a way to evaluate the health of a country's economy. Twenty-five percent of all employees in the world live and work in China. China's economy is second only to the United States.

1946

- Civil war between communists and Chiang Kai-shek begins, and millions die of starvation

1949

- Mao Zedong declares the People's Republic of China

CLOSE-UP

Elderly Rights

Elderly people are treated well in China. Families take care of older members as a sign of respect for their age and wisdom. China has an Elderly Rights Law that makes sure older people get the respect they deserve.

HISTORICAL  HIGHLIGHT

Boy vs Girl

Until China ended its one-child rule, most families hoped their unborn child would be a boy. Now, there are currently 100 million more males than females in China. Why would parents hope for a boy? Reasons included carrying on the family name and the tradition that sons are responsible for taking care of elderly parents. The idea that a son is "better" than a daughter is changing. Women in China typically have jobs and can help care for their parents. With the one-child rule gone, Chinese families welcome babies of either gender.

1966

- Cultural Revolution begins

1972

- American president Richard Nixon visits China

CLOSE-UP

Fireworks

Fireworks were invented in China more than 2,000 years ago. The first fireworks were bamboo stalks that would explode with a bang when thrown in fire. The Chinese believed that these fireworks would ward off evil spirits.

CHAPTER THREE

PEOPLE AND CULTURE

People living in China today are part of a culture that honors tradition and looks forward to the future. Chinese families are important. It is not unusual for three generations made up of grandparents, parents, and children to live together. Chinese families honor older generations and expect younger people to follow the family's rules. Children work hard in school and spend a lot of time studying and doing homework.

Teenagers don't have a lot of freedom and seldom date. Middle schools and high schools usually have rules that forbid dating between students. High school students are still considered children by adults. Parents and teachers monitor what children do. Most young people have friends of the same sex and when they get together, they play sports, go to the movies, or watch television.

People in China might live in a small town or a huge city. Wherever they live, they are known to have generous natures and are willing to share whatever they have with others. When it comes to communication, people

1989

- Tiananmen Square Massacre

1992

- Russia and China sign declaration restoring friendly relationship are often very direct. Chinese people tend to be honest and to the point. They are curious about other people and cultures and like to learn how people live and what they think.

Popular sports include basketball, badminton, and soccer. Basketball is by far the sport most people like to watch. At home, table tennis is the number one recreational sport. Almost all homes and schools have a table tennis set.

China has seven official holidays. The biggest holiday is Chinese New Year, which is celebrated on the first day in the first lunar month. This falls in January or February. Chinese New Year is the longest public holiday and usually lasts 15 days. During that time there are fireworks, parades, and huge feasts. Family reunions are often held, and people spend time at home eating, talking, and enjoying each other's company.

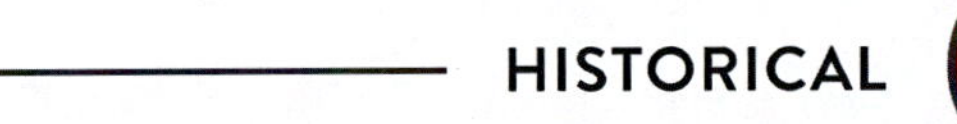
HISTORICAL  **HIGHLIGHT**

Cleaning House

Two weeks before the Chinese New Year, it's time to clean the house. Floors are washed, furniture is dusted, and kitchens are scrubbed. While it is usually the female parent in charge of cleaning, sometimes the whole family helps out. Getting rid of old dirt and dust is how the household prepares for the good fortune of the coming new year. Once the house is sparkling clean, it is decorated with red paper lanterns and red window cutouts. Now the home is ready to welcome the new year!

1999

- 50th anniversary of People's Republic of China on October 1

2003

- Launch of China's first manned spacecraft

The people of China study hard, work hard, and enjoy their free time. They look out for each other, knowing they share both the past and the future. Living in China means having to follow the rules of the government. It also means being part of a culture that has become an important player on the world's stage.

CLOSE-UP

Forbidden City

China has one of the largest palaces in the world. The Forbidden City in Beijing has 9,000 rooms. It is more than 600 years old and is one of the oldest imperial palaces in the world.

HISTORICAL HIGHLIGHT

Positive and Negative Foods

The Chinese believe there is positive energy and negative energy in the universe. "Yin" is negative, and "yang" is positive. Food groups are considered yin and yang, too. Some yin foods are soybeans, coconuts, ice cream, and oysters. Yang foods include garlic, eggplant, turkey, and beef. Both food groups must be evenly balanced to create a healthy state. Most Chinese families shop daily for fresh food. Seafood, meats, and fruits and vegetables that are in season are bought at local markets and cooked the same day.

2020

- Coronavirus (Covid-19) pandemic begins in Wuhan and quickly spreads worldwide

2022

- Beijing hosts the Winter Olympic Games

HSBC

CHAPTER FOUR

CHINA TODAY

For a long time, China was a very isolated country. The rest of the world knew very little about China and less about the people living there. Napoleon Bonaparte, the famous emperor of France, is credited with saying, "China is a sleeping giant, when she wakes, she will shake the world." Since the 1970s, China has been waking up and is shaking the world.

China has a strong economy and is a top exporter to the United States and Japan. Selling goods to other countries is a key factor in China's growth. Factories in China make everything from clothing to electronic machinery. China also exports agricultural products, plastics, and furniture. China has been called "the world's factory" because it makes and exports so many products.

However, even though China makes a lot of items, there are downsides to its productivity. Chinese workers usually don't make as much money as factory workers in other countries. Safety rules sometimes aren't enforced. Pollution standards are not as high in China as they are elsewhere. While making so many items is good for the country's economy, there are still challenges to address.

CLOSE-UP

Zodiac

Years in China are named after one of the 12 Chinese zodiac animals. The animals are rat, ox, tiger, rabbit, dragon, snake, horse, goat, monkey, rooster, dog, and pig.

Another problem in China is a large part of the country's population is getting older. Many older people can't work as hard as younger people and must be taken care of, either in their home or in an assisted living home. How to care for its older people is an issue China is dealing with.

There has always been a wide gap between people living in rural areas and those who call cities their home. People living in rural areas have fewer opportunities than people living in cities. They have less access to healthcare, and often their schools aren't as up to date as schools in cities. How to make that gap smaller is an ongoing challenge for China.

Keeping pace with the rest of the world is another goal. China began its space program in the 1950s and became the third nation to send a human into space in 2003. Growing the space program for future generations is one of China's many goals.

The Chinese people are known for their resourcefulness. Their history shows they are able to deal with obstacles and come up with creative solutions for everyday problems. How they will work as a global partner, and how the rest of the world will work with China, remains to be seen.

神箭
中国航天
CZ-2F

华夏风采
豫園禮品
上海制扇
66
64
64

ALL ABOUT

CHINA

Continent: Asia

Capital: Beijing

Population: 1.4 billion

Official language: Mandarin

Type of government: Communist state

Currency: Renminbi, commonly called the yuan

Main religion practiced: No main religion, Buddhism practiced by 18%

Colors on flag: Red and yellow

National flower: Peony

WORDS to Know

authoritarian enforcing strict obedience to authority, especially the government

commune a group of people living together and sharing possessions and responsibilities

communist a type of government and economic system in which goods are owned in common and available to all as needed

dynasty a line of hereditary rulers of a country

famine a very great shortage of food that affects many people over a wide area

Gross Domestic Product (GDP) the total value of goods produced and services provided in a country during one year

martial law the law applied by military forces in occupied territory or in an emergency

movable type a printing method where one small block is used for each character, making it easier to reproduce documents

overpopulation the condition of being populated with very large numbers

republic form of government in which a country is ruled by representatives of the citizen body

LEARN MORE

Books

Davies, Monika. *Yangtze River.* Minneapolis, MN: Bellwether Media, 2025.

Lilley, Matt. *Great Wall of China.* Mankato, MN: Creative Education and Creative Paperbacks, 2025.

Lynch, Seth. *Ancient China.* Buffalo, New York: Enslow Publishing, 2025.

Websites

"China Facts." Kids Travel Guide.

https://www.kids-world-travel-guide.com/china-facts.html

"China." History for Kids.

https://www.historyforkids.net/ancient-china.html

"China." National Geographic Kids.

https://kids.nationalgeographic.com/geography/countries/article/china

Documentaries

Bremmer, Ian, dir. *The Great Wall of China: The Hidden Story.* New York, NY, 2017.

Carr, Patrick, prod. *The Story of China.* London, UK, 2017.

Lu, Chuan, dir. *Born in China.* Shanghai, China, 2016.

Note: Every effort has been made to ensure that any websites listed above were active at the time of publication. However, because of the nature of the Internet, it is impossible to guarantee that these sites will remain active indefinitely or that their contents will not be altered.

Visit

CHIMELONG SAFARI PARK

If you want to see pandas, head to Chimelong Safari Park. The park has many different animals in addition to pandas, including giraffes and zebras.

593 Xiangjiang Blvd, Guangdong Province
Guangzhou, Panyu District 105, China

GREAT WALL OF CHINA

The Great Wall stretches across northern China. Walk along the ancient wall, explore watchtowers, and enjoy amazing views of the mountains and countryside.

Huairou District, Beijing, China

FORBIDDEN CITY

Stroll through an enormous palace with more than 9,000 rooms. Built in the 15th century, the Forbidden City is now a museum showcasing China's history and culture.

4 Jingshan Front St
Dong Cheng Qu
Bei Jing Shi, China 100009

MUSEUM OF QIN TERRA-COTTA

Interested in archaeology? Visit the Museum of Qin Terra-cotta Warriors and Horses and see more than 7,000 life-size terracotta figures that were originally buried with Emperor Qin Shi Huang.

Qinling North Road
Linton District, Xi'an, China

INDEX